SCHOLASTIC
studySMART

Grammar Builder

Level 1
English

Copyright © 2013 Scholastic Education International (Singapore) Private Limited
All rights reserved.

Previously published as Success with Grammer series by Scholastic Inc.

This edition published by Scholastic Education International (Singapore) Private Limited
A division of Scholastic Inc.

No part of this publication may be reproduced in whole or in part, or stored in a retrieval system, or transmitted in any form or by any means, electronic, mechanical, photocopying, recording, or otherwise without the written permission of the publisher. For information regarding permission, write to:
Scholastic Education International (Singapore) Private Limited
81 Ubi Avenue 4 #02-28 UB.ONE Singapore 408830
education@scholastic.com.sg

First edition 2013

ISBN 978-981-07-5256-9

Welcome to studySMART!

Grammar Builder lets your child review and apply essential grammar rules.

Knowledge of grammar is essential in ensuring your child understands the patterns and rules in the English language. As your child progresses through the practice worksheets, he will strengthen the skills needed to read and write well.

Grammar items covered in one level are reinforced at the subsequent level. This helps to ensure that your child consolidates his learning of a particular grammar item and builds upon it.

Each grammar item is covered in three pages. The first two pages target your child's ability to identify and apply the grammar item. The third page provides a quick assessment of your child's understanding of the use of the grammar item. A revision section at the end of the book also allows for easy assessment of your child's understanding of the grammar items covered in each workbook.

How to use this book?

1. Introduce the target grammar item at the top of the page to your child.

2. Direct your child's attention to the grammar box to review the grammar rule.

3. Let your child complete the practices independently.

4. Use the Assessment pages and Revision section to evaluate your child's understanding of the grammar items.

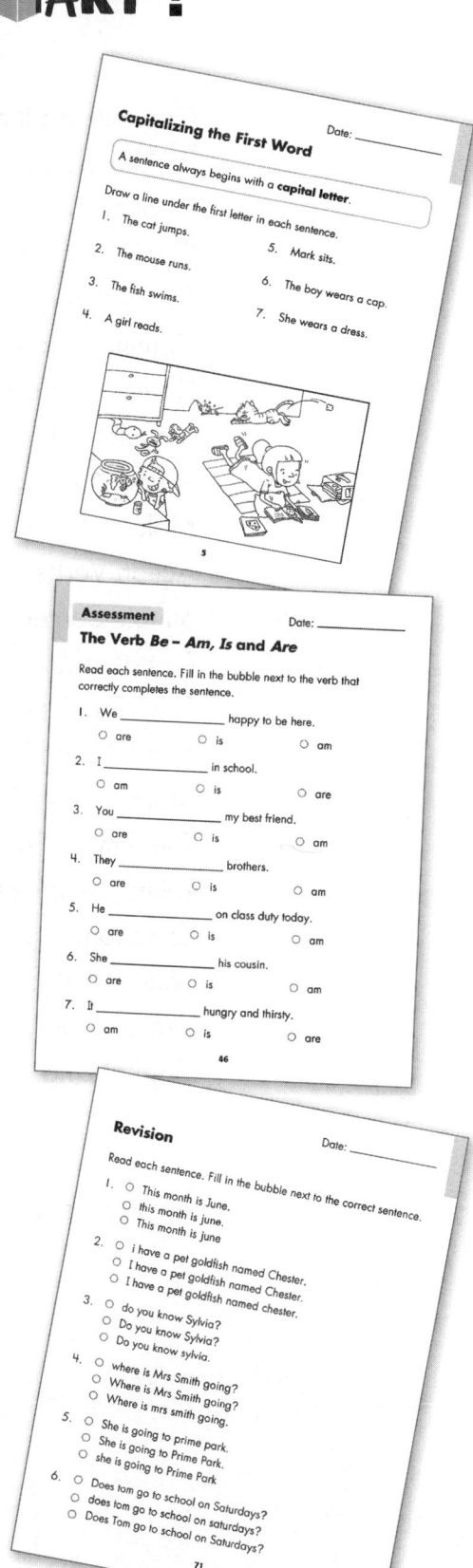

Contents

Capitalizing the First Word 5–7
Periods 8–10
Capitalizing I... 11–13
Capitalizing Months and Days 14–16
Capitalizing Special Names 17–19
Common Nouns 20–22
Common and Proper Nouns 23–25
Singular and Plural Nouns.............................. 26–28
A and An 29–31
Male or Female.. 32–34
Action Verbs 35–37
Simple Sentences 38–40
Pronouns 41–43
The Verb Be – Am, Is and Are 44–46
More Action Verbs 47–49
More Simple Sentences 50–52
The Simple Present Tense 53–55
Telling Sentences 56–58
Questions 59–61
Question Words... 62–64
Word Order... 65–67
Capitalizing Names and First Words 68–70
Revision 71–76

Answer Key... 77–80

Date: _____

Capitalizing the First Word

A sentence always begins with a **capital letter**.

Draw a line under the first letter in each sentence.

1. The cat jumps.

2. The mouse runs.

3. The fish swims.

4. A girl reads.

5. Mark sits.

6. The boy wears a cap.

7. She wears a dress.

5

Date: _____

Capitalizing the First Word

Copy each sentence correctly on the line.

1. the cat sat on the mat.

   _____

2. the girl runs.

   _____

3. i can see a mouse.

   _____

4. the dog sees the cat.

   _____

5. i see a boy.

   _____

6. the cat sleeps.

   _____

Assessment

Date: _____

Capitalizing the First Word

Complete each sentence. Fill in the bubble next to the correct word with the capital letter.

1. _____ cat is in the van.

    ○ The ○ the

2. _____ likes juice.

    ○ Jan ○ jan

3. _____ like jam.

    ○ ants ○ Ants

4. _____ dog can run.

    ○ my ○ My

5. _____ like bread.

    ○ I ○ i

6. _____ likes milk.

    ○ Snuffles ○ snuffles

7

Date: _____

Periods

> A **telling sentence** ends with a **period**.

Circle the period at the end of each sentence.

1. I see Danny.

2. I see Tina.

3. We walk to school.

4. We like school.

Copy each sentence correctly on the line.

5. I go to school with Tina

_____

6. Tina is my friend

_____

7. Danny is our friend

_____

Date: _____

Periods

Put a period where it belongs in each sentence.

1. I like school

2. I meet Danny in school

3. Tina is my classmate

4. We go to the same class

Copy each sentence correctly on the line. Put the period in the correct place.

5. I have fun. in school

   _____

6. We. play games in school

   _____

7. I like my. teachers

   _____

Assessment

Date: _____

Periods

Read each group of words. Fill in the bubble next to the correct sentence.

1. ○ Miss Gray is my teacher
   ○ miss Gray is my teacher.
   ○ Miss Gray is my teacher.

2. ○ School is fun
   ○ School is fun.
   ○ school is fun.

3. ○ I like the playground
   ○ I like the playground.
   ○ i like the playground.

4. ○ Tina and I like the see-saw
   ○ Tina and I like the see-saw.
   ○ tina and I like the see-saw.

5. ○ danny likes the swing
   ○ danny likes the swing.
   ○ Danny likes the swing.

Date: _____

Capitalizing *I*

Always write the word ***I*** with a capital letter.

Circle the word *I* in each sentence.

1. I can run.

2. I can jump.

3. Grace and I can skip.

4. Kevin and I can hop.

Read the sentences. Write *I* on each blank.

5. _____ can ride a bicycle.

6. _____ like to swim.

7. Mom and _____ like to sing.

8. Dad and _____ like to read.

11

Date: _____

Capitalizing *I*

Copy each sentence correctly on the line. Remember to capitalize the word *I*.

1. i like to read.

   _____

2. i can hop and i can jump.

   _____

3. My brother and i like to swim.

   _____

4. Jake and i have fun together.

   _____

What do you like? Write two sentences starting with *I like*. Remember to capitalize the word *I*.

_____

_____

_____

Assessment

Date: _____

Capitalizing *I*

Read each group of words. Fill in the bubble next to the correct sentence.

1. ○ i have fun in the sun.
   ○ I have fun in the sun.
   ○ I have fun in the sun

2. ○ Jake and i play with the beach ball.
   ○ Jake and I play with the beach ball.
   ○ jake and i play with the beach ball

3. ○ I like the beach
   ○ i like the beach.
   ○ I like the beach.

4. ○ Peter and i build sandcastles.
   ○ peter and I build sandcastles
   ○ Peter and I build sandcastles.

5. ○ My dog and i run on the sand.
   ○ my dog and i run on the sand.
   ○ My dog and I run on the sand.

Date: _____

Capitalizing Months and Days

> The months of the year and the days of the week always begin with a capital letter.

Write the months of the year correctly.

january	_____	july	_____
february	_____	august	_____
march	_____	september	_____
april	_____	october	_____
may	_____	november	_____
june	_____	december	_____

Complete the calendar below with the days of the week. Remember to use capital letters.

sunday	friday	thursday
wednesday	saturday	tuesday

_____, 2 April	_____, 5 April
Monday, 3 April	_____, 6 April
	_____, 7 April
_____, 4 April	_____, 8 April

Date: _____

Capitalizing Months and Days

Copy each sentence correctly on the line. Remember to capitalize the months and days.

1. I start school on monday, 3 january.

   _____

2. My brother's birthday is in august.

   _____

3. We visit my grandparents every sunday.

   _____

4. The months of june and july are very warm.

   _____

5. We will celebrate my birthday on a saturday in september.

   _____

   _____

Assessment

Date: _____

Capitalizing Months and Days

Look at the calendar below. Then, complete the sentences with the correct month or day.

January						
Sunday	Monday	Tuesday	Wednesday	Thursday	Friday	Saturday
	1	2	3	4	5	

January						
Sunday	Monday	Tuesday	Wednesday	Thursday	Friday	Saturday
		1	2	3	4	5
6	7	8	9	10	11	12
13	14	15	16	17	18	19
20	21	22	23	24	25	26
27	28	29	30	31		

February						
Sunday	Monday	Tuesday	Wednesday	Thursday	Friday	Saturday
					1	2
3	4	5	6	7	8	9
10	11	12	13	14	15	16
17	18	19	20	21	22	23
24	25	26	27	28		

1. 3 January is a _____.

2. 23 January is a _____.

3. 28 _____ is a Thursday.

4. 5 and 12 _____ are Saturdays.

5. 24 February is a _____.

6. 19 February is a _____.

Date: _____

Capitalizing Special Names

> The names of people, places and pets are special. They begin with capital letters.

Draw a line under the special name in each sentence. Then, circle the first letter or letters in that name.

1. Dan and Jan go to Hill Park.

2. They bring their pet cat Felix.

3. They like to go to Grange Lake.

4. Grange Lake is in Hill Park.

Copy each sentence correctly on the line. Remember to capitalize each special name.

5. My dog is buster and my cat is felix.

   _____

6. My brother's name is gary and I am sue.

   _____

7. We stay on margaret drive.

   _____

17

Date: _____

Capitalizing Special Names

Complete each sentence with a special name. Use the words in the box to help you. Remember to capitalize the special names.

| anne | candy road | jim |
| sweet house | snowball | |

1. My name is _____ and I am a girl.

2. I have a brother and his name is _____.

3. My pet cat is white and fluffy. I call her _____.

4. We live on _____.

5. I like to go to the candy shop near my house. The name of the shop is _____.

Complete the sentences below with your own words.

6. My name is _____.

7. I live on _____.

8. My school is called _____.

18

Assessment   Date: _____

Capitalizing Special Names

Read each sentence. Fill in the bubble next to each special name.

1. Can Don and Marie go to the picnic?
   ○ Don   ○ Can   ○ Marie

2. The picnic will be on Pink Hill.
   ○ The   ○ picnic   ○ Pink Hill

3. They will bring their pets Mopy and Dopy.
   ○ They   ○ Mopy   ○ Dopy

4. Pink Hill is on Jam Street.
   ○ Pink Hill   ○ Jam Street   ○ is

5. Don and Marie will meet James there.
   ○ Don   ○ Marie   ○ James

6. They asked James to bring his pet rabbit.
   ○ They   ○ rabbit   ○ James

Date: _____

Common Nouns

> **Common nouns** name people, places and things, for example, a man, a house or a table.

Read each sentence. Draw a line under the word or words that name the person, place or thing in each sentence.

1. The boys live in a big house.

2. They have many toys.

3. They play with their toys in the garden.

4. The garden is at the front of the house.

5. They have a sister.

Draw a line from each sentence to the picture that shows the naming word in that sentence.

6. The sun is hot.

7. The cat is big and fat.

8. The house is very dirty.

Date: _____

Common Nouns

Circle the common nouns in each sentence.

1. We can go in a van.

2. The cat sat on a mat.

3. They ran up the hill.

4. They had a picnic.

Draw a picture of a person, place or thing. Write a sentence about your picture. Circle the naming word or words.

_____

_____

Assessment

Common Nouns

Date: _____

Read each sentence. Fill in the bubble next to each common noun.

1. I see a big cat.

    ○ see   ○ big   ○ cat

2. The rat ran fast.

    ○ rat   ○ ran   ○ fast

3. Can you see the map?

    ○ can   ○ map   ○ see

4. The van is brown.

    ○ is   ○ van   ○ brown

5. The fan is not on!

    ○ not   ○ fan   ○ on

6. Where is the house?

    ○ is   ○ the   ○ house

Date: _____

Common and Proper Nouns

> **Common nouns** name people, places and things. They do not begin with a capital letter. **Proper nouns** have special names and begin with capital letters.

Complete the table below with the correct common or proper nouns.

house	Anna	teacher	lake
rabbit	Buster	rose	flower
Park Lane	cat	Jake	mother
Janice	Rigby Garden	mat	City Beach

Common Nouns	Proper Nouns

Think of other common nouns or proper nouns to add to your table.

Date: _____

Common and Proper Nouns

Read each sentence. Circle each common noun. Underline each proper noun.

1. James and John are friends.

2. They share their toys and food.

3. They stay in the same block along Cross Street.

4. They go to Cameron Primary School together.

5. Both James and John have pet dogs.

6. They bring their dogs to the park near their block.

7. The park is called Hyde Park.

Assessment   Date: _____

Common and Proper Nouns

Read each sentence. Fill in the bubble next to each common noun.

1. Felix the cat is very fat.
   - ○ Felix
   - ○ fat
   - ○ cat

2. Felix likes to eat fish.
   - ○ Felix
   - ○ eat
   - ○ fish

3. Felix likes to hide under the bed.
   - ○ hide
   - ○ under
   - ○ bed

Read each sentence. Fill in the bubble next to each proper noun.

4. Mary stays in a very small house.
   - ○ Mary
   - ○ small
   - ○ house

5. Her house is on Maxwell Road.
   - ○ on
   - ○ house
   - ○ Maxwell Road

6. Her younger sister is Rose.
   - ○ Rose
   - ○ sister
   - ○ younger

Date: _____

Singular and Plural Nouns

> Many nouns, or naming words, add **-s** to show more than one.

Match the singular nouns with the plural nouns.

1. cat   boys
2. girl   pencils
3. boy   girls
4. egg   books
5. pencil   eggs
6. book   cats
7. bag   cars
8. car   bags

Read each sentence. Draw a line under each naming word that means more than one.

9. Jane has a bag and two hats.

10. She has two dolls.

11. They have two eyes and two ears.

12. They have nice skirts.

Date: _____

Singular and Plural Nouns

Look at each picture. Read each word. Write the plural naming word that matches the picture.

1. cat _____

2. bag _____

3. cap _____

4. book _____

5. ball _____

6. car _____

27

Assessment

Date: _____

Singular and Plural Nouns

Read each sentence. Fill in the bubble next to each noun that means one.

1. The girl has two pets.

    ○ girl ○ has ○ pets

2. They share a cake and some sweets.

    ○ They ○ cake ○ sweets

3. There are two beds in the room.

    ○ beds ○ two ○ room

Read each sentence. Fill in the bubble next to each noun that means more than one.

4. Mary sees a cup and two spoons.

    ○ Mary ○ cup ○ spoons

5. She takes out two plates and bowls.

    ○ plates ○ bowls ○ takes

6. She finds a table and two chairs.

    ○ finds ○ table ○ chairs

Date: _____

A and An

We use **a** or **an** with a singular noun. We use **an** for most nouns that begin with a vowel, for example, a cat, an owl.

Write *a* or *an* before each noun.

1. _____ mat

2. _____ bowl

3. _____ table

4. _____ owl

5. _____ ant

6. _____ egg

7. _____ octopus

8. _____ ice cream

Date: _____

A and An

There is a mistake in each sentence. Can you spot it?
Copy each sentence correctly on the line.

1. I see a owl in a tree.

   _____

2. She cracked a egg into a bowl.

   _____

3. We sit in an car and sing a song.

   _____

4. May I have a ice cream and a waffle, please?

   _____

   _____

5. He wants a umbrella and a raincoat.

   _____

   _____

30

Assessment

Date: _____

A and An

Read each sentence. Fill in blanks with *a* or *an*.

1. Mark has _____ hamster.

2. His hamster has _____ wheel.

3. His hamster eats _____ cracker.

4. Mark puts his hamster in _____ cage.

5. Mark eats _____ egg for breakfast.

6. Mark drinks _____ cup of tea.

7. He gives his hamster _____ tray of water.

8. He sees _____ ant in the water.

Date: _____

Male or Female

> **Masculine nouns** name male nouns. **Feminine nouns** name female nouns.

Complete the table below with the correct nouns.

boy	king	prince	waiter	father
girl	man	princess	woman	queen
mother	son	waitress	daughter	uncle
actor	aunt	nephew	actress	niece

Masculine Nouns	**Feminine Nouns**

Can you think of other male or female nouns to add to your table?

Date: _____

Male or Female

Look at the picture. This is a picture of Sally's family. Can you put in the correct nouns for each of her family members? Use the words in the box to help you.

| grandfather | grandmother | mother |
| father | brother | sister |

33

Assessment

Date: _____

Male or Female

Read the sentences and look at the pictures. Fill in the blanks with the correct male or female noun.

1. The _____ dances with the prince.

2. The _____ serves the food.

3. My mother's mother is my _____.

4. He is the famous _____ from the movie.

5. That _____ is wearing the cap his sister gave him.

34

Date: _____

Action Verbs

> An **action verb** tells what happens.

Read each sentence. Circle the word that tells what happens.

1. Peter jumps onto the chair.

2. Jack slides all the way down.

3. Josie and Karen play on the see-saw.

4. Maggie sits on the swing.

5. David swings on the monkey bars.

6. Joe and Gus skip together.

7. Steven climbs the ladder.

8. The cat sleeps on the merry-go-round.

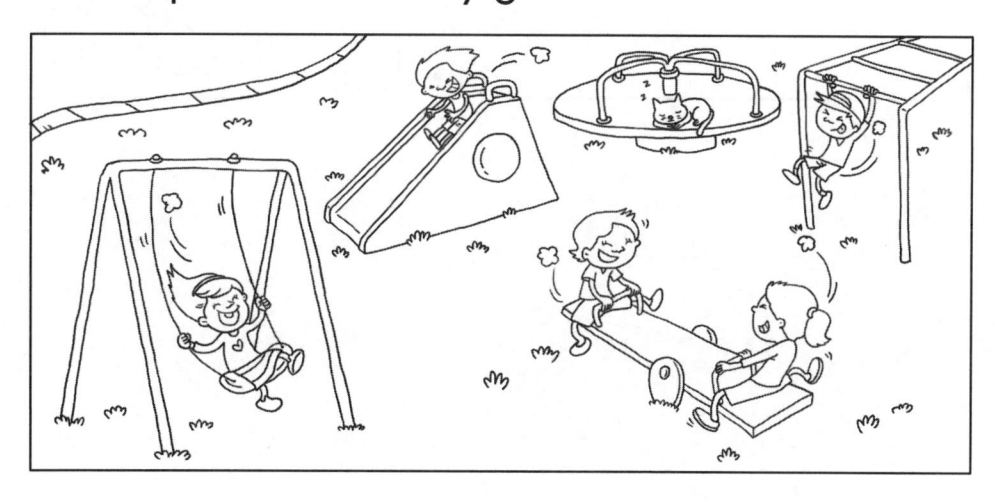

Action Verbs

Complete the sentences. Use the words in the box to help you.

| sweeps | mops | sit |
| runs | wipes | |

1. The boy _____.

2. Mary _____ the floor.

3. They _____ on the couch.

4. Joseph _____ the table.

5. Mother _____ the floor.

Assessment

Date: _____

Action Verbs

Read the sentences. Fill in the bubble next to the action verb.

1. I sit on the chair.

    ○ sit ○ chair ○ I

2. The mouse runs up the clock.

    ○ mouse ○ runs ○ clock

3. She sleeps on the bed.

    ○ she ○ sleeps ○ bed

4. The cat digs up sand.

    ○ cat ○ digs ○ sand

5. They play in the playground.

    ○ they ○ play ○ playground

6. Jack walks to the park.

    ○ walks ○ Jack ○ park

Date: _____

Simple Sentences

> A **sentence** is a group of words that tells a complete idea.

Circle each sentence.

1. The cat
   The cat jumps.

2. The bus moves quickly.
   The bus

3. Bill
   Bill paints a picture.

4. likes to read
   Tom likes to read.

5. plant flowers
   Jessie plants flowers.

Date: _____

Simple Sentences

Arrange the words correctly. Write each sentence correctly on the line. Remember to use a period at the end of each sentence.

1. Janet   a book   reads

   _____

2. Jack   up the hill   walks

   _____

3. The   elephant   slowly   moves

   _____

4. after the cat   The dog   chases

   _____

5. looks   He   at the boy

   _____

6. Maggie   sleeps   on the bed

   _____

Assessment

Date: _____

Simple Sentences

Read each group of words. Fill in the bubble next to the complete sentence.

1. ○ The cat
   ○ The cat sits on a mat.
   ○ on a mat

2. ○ The girls like jam.
   ○ The girls
   ○ like jam

3. ○ Jacob
   ○ Jacob eats a banana.
   ○ eats a banana.

4. ○ Thomas walks to school.
   ○ Thomas
   ○ walks to school

5. ○ plucks flowers
   ○ Jessie plucks flowers.
   ○ Jessie

Date: _____

Pronouns

> A **pronoun** takes the place of the name of a person, place or thing.

Read each pair of sentences. Circle the pronoun in the second sentence of each pair. Then, write what the pronoun stands for. The first one has been done for you.

1. Wendell did not like to clean his room.
   (He) liked a messy room.   <u>Wendell</u>

2. Mother wanted Wendell to do some work.
   She handed Wendell a broom.   _____

3. The Carrolls came into Wendell's room.
   They helped Wendell clean the room.   _____

4. Wendell and the Carrolls played a game.
   They had fun playing it.   _____

5. The Carrolls and Wendell played for hours.
   They liked to play games.   _____

6. Wendell was sad to see his friends go.
   He liked playing with the Carrolls.   _____

Date: _____

Pronouns

Complete the sentences. Use the pronouns in the box to help you.

| they | he | she | it |

1. Glenda walked in the woods and saw a house. _____ was empty.

2. She opened the door and saw three chairs by the fireplace. _____ were all of different sizes.

3. Glenda sat on the smallest chair. _____ was the perfect size for her.

4. Glenda fell asleep. When _____ woke up, she saw three bears standing over her.

5. The father bear spoke. _____ asked Glenda to stay for dinner.

Assessment   Date: _____

Pronouns

Read each sentence. Fill in the bubble next to the word or words that the underlined pronoun stands for.

1. <u>She</u> did not like the room to be messy.

    ○ Max   ○ The cat   ○ Max's mother

2. <u>He</u> did not like to sweep the floor.

    ○ Max   ○ The girl   ○ Max's mother

3. <u>It</u> was full of books and dirty clothes.

    ○ The room   ○ Max   ○ Max's cat

Read each sentence. Fill in the bubble next to the pronoun that can take the place of the underlined word or words.

4. <u>Mary</u> waved goodbye to her friends.

    ○ He   ○ She   ○ It   ○ They

5. Joe hoped that <u>Meg and Ben</u> would come back.

    ○ He   ○ She   ○ It   ○ They

6. <u>Jim</u> likes to swim in the sea.

    ○ He   ○ She   ○ It   ○ They

7. <u>The monkey</u> swings from branch to branch.

    ○ He   ○ She   ○ It   ○ They

The Verb *Be* – *Am*, *Is* and *Are*

Am, *is* and *are* are forms of the verb *be*. They are not action verbs.

Read each sentence. Write the verb on the line.

1. The story is perfect. _____

2. The producers are happy. _____

3. The actors are funny. _____

4. The movie studio is interested in the story. _____

5. I am excited about the movie. _____

Date: _____

The Verb *Be* – *Am*, *Is* and *Are*

> We use **am** with the pronoun **I** and **is** with singular nouns or the pronouns **he**, **she** or **it**. We use **are** with plural nouns or the pronouns **you**, **we** or **they**.

Choose a verb from the box to complete each sentence.

am	is	are

1. The movie _____ long.

2. She _____ at the movies.

3. They _____ at the movie theater.

4. The producers _____ happy with the movie.

5. I _____ at the theater with my friends.

6. The actors _____ at the opening night.

7. You _____ the lead actress!

8. He _____ the producer of the movie.

Assessment Date: _____

The Verb *Be* – *Am, Is* and *Are*

Read each sentence. Fill in the bubble next to the verb that correctly completes the sentence.

1. We _____ happy to be here.

   ○ are   ○ is   ○ am

2. I _____ in school.

   ○ am   ○ is   ○ are

3. You _____ my best friend.

   ○ are   ○ is   ○ am

4. They _____ brothers.

   ○ are   ○ is   ○ am

5. He _____ on class duty today.

   ○ are   ○ is   ○ am

6. She _____ his cousin.

   ○ are   ○ is   ○ am

7. It _____ hungry and thirsty.

   ○ am   ○ is   ○ are

46

More Action Verbs

> A **verb** tells what someone or something is doing.

Read each sentence. Circle the verb.

1. Maggie eats her cereal and drinks her milk.

2. Grace opens the box of sandwiches.

3. Joyce and Meg sip their orange juice.

4. The ants march towards the jam.

5. The cat chases after a butterfly.

6. David plays ball with Sam.

7. A snake slithers along the grass.

8. Sue screams when she sees the snake.

Date: _____

More Action Verbs

Complete each sentence with an action verb from the box.

| jumps | slides | runs | sleep | eat |
| drinks | sits | kick | play | walk |

1. Jacob _____ up and down and bounces on the trampoline.

2. The boy _____ in a race.

3. Meg _____ down the water slide and has a whale of a time.

4. The children _____ in their beds.

5. The cat _____ its milk from a tray.

6. The boys _____ a football at the field.

7. Chris and Andy _____ along the road.

8. Can you _____ the whole plate of food?

9. The girls _____ with their dolls.

10. Cary _____ in his rocking chair.

Assessment Date: _____

More Action Verbs

Read each sentence. Fill in the bubble next to the action verb.

1. He kicks the ball into the net.
   ○ He   ○ kicks   ○ net

2. They cycle all the way to the pier.
   ○ They   ○ cycle   ○ pier

3. She throws the rubbish away.
   ○ She   ○ rubbish   ○ throws

4. The frog hops onto the lily pad.
   ○ The frog   ○ hops   ○ lily pad

5. I wash the plates and the cups.
   ○ wash   ○ plates   ○ cups

6. You sit in the big chair.
   ○ You   ○ sit   ○ chair

Date: _____

More Simple Sentences

> The **subject** of a sentence is the person or thing doing the action. The **object** is the person or thing the subject does something to.

Read each sentence. Underline the subject in each sentence. The first one has been done for you.

1. <u>Patty</u> mixes the ingredients.

2. George kneads the dough.

3. May spoons out the dough.

4. Alex puts the tray in the oven.

Read each sentence. Circle the object in each sentence. The first one has been done for you.

5. Chris throws (the rubbish).

6. Alina drinks juice.

7. Tina sweeps the floor.

8. Belle cleans the table.

Date: _____

More Simple Sentences

Read each sentence. Underline the subject and circle the object in each sentence.

1. Mr Tuck reads the newspapers.

2. Mrs Tuck makes breakfast.

3. Mary pours the juice.

4. Alex sets the table.

5. Margie feeds the rabbit.

6. The rabbit eats the carrots.

7. Baby Boo drinks his milk.

8. Baby Sue throws the rattle.

Now, write a sentence with a subject and an object.

_____

_____

Assessment

More Simple Sentences

Date: _____

Read each sentence. Fill in the bubble next to a complete sentence.

1. ○ The man
   ○ The man rocks the boat.
   ○ rocks the boat

2. ○ She
   ○ kicks the pail
   ○ She kicks the pail.

3. ○ They
   ○ They bake bread.
   ○ bake bread

4. ○ Mrs Kim stirs the soup.
   ○ stirs the soup
   ○ Mrs Kim

5. ○ Mr Wendell
   ○ Mr Wendell moves the furniture.
   ○ moves the furniture

6. ○ Adam
   ○ plays his guitar
   ○ Adam plays his guitar.

Date: _____

The Simple Present Tense

We use the **simple present tense** to talk about something that is happening now.

Read each sentence. Fill in the bubble next to the word in the simple present tense.

1. Mark is the best student in this school.
   ○ is   ○ student   ○ school

2. The cows eat all day long.
   ○ eat   ○ the cows   ○ day

3. The farmer milks the cow in the morning.
   ○ the cow   ○ milks   ○ the farmer

4. Ginny wears a coat.
   ○ Ginny   ○ coat   ○ wears

5. She keeps her books in her bag.
   ○ keeps   ○ books   ○ bag

6. Mum irons the clothes.
   ○ Mum   ○ clothes   ○ irons

7. Dad drives his car to work.
   ○ Dad   ○ car   ○ drives

Date: _____

The Simple Present Tense

Complete the story. Use the words in the box to help you.

| trains | is | drinks | catches |
| helps | bats | eats | jogs |

Janet 1. _____ the captain of the team. She

2. _____ every day. She 3. _____ very well and is one of the best batters in her team. She has big hands and 4. _____ the ball easily. Janet

5. _____ her team members when they have problems. She also 6. _____ around the track to keep fit.

Janet 7. _____ a lot of water and

8. _____ a lot of fruits and vegetables to stay healthy. We should follow her example.

54

Assessment   Date: _____

The Simple Present Tense

Complete each sentence with the simple present tense of the verb in brackets.

1. Rob _____ (sing) at his school concert.

2. His brother, Tom, _____ (play) the guitar.

3. The audience _____ (clap) their hands.

4. Rob and Tom _____ (win) the top prize.

5. Their classmates _____ (stand) up for them.

6. Sue, their sister, _____ (give) them flowers.

7. Their parents _____ (be) proud of them.

8. They _____ (get) a trophy.

9. The principal _____ (present) the prize.

10. She _____ (shake) their hands.

Date: _____

Telling Sentences

A **telling sentence** makes a statement. Remember that a telling sentence starts with a capital letter and ends with a period.

Draw a line under the capital letter at the beginning of each telling sentence. Then, circle the period at the end of each telling sentence.

1. I see the basket.

2. The cat is in the basket.

3. We can put the hats in the basket.

4. The socks can go in too.

Draw a line under each telling sentence.

5. I can fill the basket.

6. Can you fill the basket?

7. We can put everything in it.

Date: _____

Telling Sentences

Copy each sentence correctly on the line. Remember to use capital letters and periods.

1. she sells shells in her shop

   _____

2. there are big shells and small shells

   _____

3. she gets them from the beach

   _____

4. she strings them to make necklaces

   _____

5. she opens her shop early in the morning

   _____

6. she closes the shop late at night

   _____

Assessment

Date: _____

Telling Sentences

Read the sentences. Fill in the bubble next to each telling sentence.

1. ○ Can you water the flowers?
   ○ You can water the flowers.

2. ○ Are the flowers blooming?
   ○ The flowers are blooming well.

3. ○ Do you have roses in your garden?
   ○ There are red and white roses in the garden.

4. ○ The flowers are beautiful.
   ○ Do you like the flowers?

5. ○ I can give you some roses.
   ○ Can I have the red roses?

6. ○ Where can I put them?
   ○ You can put them in the vase.

7. ○ Do you have other plants in your garden?
   ○ I have fruit trees too.

8. ○ I have apple trees and lemon trees.
   ○ Can I have some lemons too?

Date: _____

Questions

> A **question** asks something. A question begins with a capital letter and ends with a question mark.

Draw a line under the capital letter at the beginning of each question. Then, circle the question mark at the end of each question.

1. Can you see the bus stop?

2. Where should I alight?

3. Who will meet me there?

4. What time should I meet you?

Draw a line under each question.

5. She stops at the cinema.

6. Is she meeting someone?

7. Who is she meeting?

Date: _____

Questions

Copy each question correctly on the line. Remember to use capital letters and question marks.

1. where are they going

   _____

2. who are they going out with

   _____

3. will they return home by dinnertime

   _____

4. what are they going to buy

   _____

5. can they buy something for me

   _____

6. do you want to go with them

   _____

Assessment

Questions

Read the sentences. Fill in the bubble next to each question.

1. ○ Where can I buy this book?
   ○ You can buy it at the bookstore.

2. ○ Do you have this book here?
   ○ I think we have this book here.

3. ○ Is this the book you want?
   ○ This is the book I want.

4. ○ How much is this book?
   ○ I have enough money for the book.

5. ○ I want to find another book.
   ○ What book are you looking for?

6. ○ I know the writer.
   ○ What is the writer's name?

7. ○ Do you have books by Lyndon Wells?
   ○ We have only one book by Lyndon Wells.

8. ○ Can I have a look at it?
   ○ Yes, of course.

Question Words

> We often use **question words** like **who**, **where**, **what**, **when** and **how** at the beginning of questions.

Draw a line under each question word.

1. What is your name?

2. Who is that man?

3. Where are you going?

4. When does school start?

5. How are you today?

Read each question. Fill in the bubble next to the words that tell what each question word is asking for.

6. Where is your school?

    ○ a place   ○ a person   ○ a date

7. Who is that woman?

    ○ a place   ○ a person   ○ a date

8. When are you going?

    ○ a place   ○ a person   ○ a date

Date: _____

Question Words

Read each set of question and answer. Complete each question with the correct question word.

1. _____ are you doing?

   I am making a kite.

2. _____ is your teacher?

   My teacher is Miss Gillis.

3. _____ are you going for your holiday?

   We are going to Japan.

4. _____ are you leaving?

   I am leaving on Tuesday.

5. _____ are you going there?

   I am going there by plane.

Assessment

Date: _____

Question Words

Read each question. Fill in the bubble next to the question word that correctly completes each question.

1. _____ shall we go to the zoo?

   ○ When   ○ Where   ○ What

2. _____ time is it?

   ○ When   ○ Where   ○ What

3. _____ is her father?

   ○ When   ○ Who   ○ What

4. _____ is Lukon Valley?

   ○ When   ○ Where   ○ Who

5. _____ do we get there?

   ○ How   ○ Where   ○ What

6. _____ will the flowers bloom?

   ○ When   ○ Who   ○ What

Date: _____

Word Order

> Words in a sentence must be in an order that makes sense.

Read each group of words. Draw a line under the words that are in an order that makes sense.

1. The king is sad.
   sad. The king is

2. Tell the king to come.
   to come. The king tell

3. Shall we cheer him up?
   we cheer him up? Shall

4. He eat cake. likes to
   He likes to eat cake.

5. Shall we bake him a cake?
   we a cake? bake him Shall

6. A strawberry cake. bake him We can
   We can bake him a strawberry cake.

65

Date: _____

Word Order

These words are mixed up. Put them in order. Then, write each sentence correctly on the line.

1. snow.   bear   likes   This

   _____

2. water   cold.   is   The

   _____

3. Can   swim?   bear   the

   _____

4. fast.   The   bear   swims

   _____

5. What   is   color   the bear?

   _____

Assessment

Date: _____

Word Order

Read each group of words. Fill in the bubble next to the words that are in an order that makes sense.

1. ○ baseball. will The boys play
   ○ The boys will play baseball.
   ○ The boys baseball. play will

2. ○ The baseball smashes the window.
   ○ smashes the window. The baseball
   ○ the window. The baseball smashes

3. ○ angry. is The teacher
   ○ is The teacher angry.
   ○ The teacher is angry.

4. ○ The teacher scolds the boys.
   ○ the boys. scolds The teacher
   ○ scolds the boys. The teacher

5. ○ sorry. The boys are
   ○ The boys are sorry.
   ○ are sorry. The boys

67

Date: _____

Capitalizing Names and First Words

> We use capital letters for the first word in sentences. We also use capital letters for words that name a person, place or thing.

Read the sentences. Circle the words that are capitalized.

1. The goats Gruff have a problem.

2. They do not like Nosey the troll.

3. Nosey is big and bad.

4. Nosey lives under Toll Bridge.

Copy the sentences correctly. Remember to use capital letters where needed.

5. her sister is named sheila.

   _____

6. they have a pet called muffins.

   _____

7. muffins stays in their house on park lane.

   _____

Date: _____

Capitalizing Names and First Words

We use capital letters for special names that name a person, place or thing.

Circle the special names in the picture. Write each one correctly on a line.

Picture labels: the sun, Gruff Park, Mr and Mrs Smith, a tree, a bird, Amy, Trevor

1. _____   3. _____

2. _____   4. _____

69

Assessment

Date: _____

Capitalizing Names and First Words

Read each sentence. Fill in the bubble next to the word that needs a capital letter.

1. I read the story with jenny.
   ○ I   ○ Story   ○ Jenny

2. the goats in the story are called the goats Gruff.
   ○ The   ○ Goats   ○ Gruff

3. Little gruff had a problem.
   ○ Little   ○ Problem   ○ Gruff

4. There was a troll called nosey on the bridge.
   ○ There   ○ Troll   ○ Nosey

5. nosey was a big, mean troll.
   ○ Big   ○ Troll   ○ Nosey

6. the goats needed to cross Toll Bridge.
   ○ The   ○ Goats   ○ Toll Bridge

Revision

Read each sentence. Fill in the bubble next to the correct sentence.

1. ○ This month is June.
   ○ this month is june.
   ○ This month is june

2. ○ i have a pet goldfish named Chester.
   ○ I have a pet goldfish named Chester.
   ○ I have a pet goldfish named chester.

3. ○ do you know Sylvia?
   ○ Do you know Sylvia?
   ○ Do you know sylvia.

4. ○ where is Mrs Smith going?
   ○ Where is Mrs Smith going?
   ○ Where is mrs smith going.

5. ○ She is going to prime park.
   ○ She is going to Prime Park.
   ○ she is going to Prime Park

6. ○ Does tom go to school on Saturdays?
   ○ does tom go to school on saturdays?
   ○ Does Tom go to school on Saturdays?

Read each sentence. Fill in the bubble next to the word that completes each sentence correctly.

7. My pet bird _____ called Peewee.
   ○ is   ○ are

8. Peewee _____ sunflower seeds.
   ○ eat   ○ eats

9. Peewee and Herman _____ siblings.
   ○ are   ○ is

10. My friend, Joe, _____ Herman.
    ○ keep   ○ keeps

11. Peewee's feathers _____ brown.
    ○ is   ○ are

12. Peewee _____ around in my house.
    ○ flies   ○ fly

13. He _____ in his cage at night.
    ○ sleep   ○ sleeps

Complete the sentences with the correct word. Circle the correct word in brackets.

14. (A / **An**) elephant is big and strong. It has (**a** / an) long trunk and big ears.

15. The son of the king is the (princess / **prince**).

16. My (niece / **nephew**) is my sister's son.

17. My (**grandfather** / grandmother) likes to go for his walk in the afternoon.

18. She has (**a** / an) cane to help her walk.

19. My mother is upset. (He / **She**) wants me to clean up my room.

20. I like to watch the ships. (It / **They**) look so grand.

21. The cat (sit / **sits**) on the mat. (**It** / They) looks around for the mouse.

22. The horses (pulls / **pull**) the wagon. (It / **They**) look so tired.

23. The boys (**run** / runs) up the hill.

Complete the sentences with the correct words. Use the words in the box to help you.

| when | where | who | how |

24. _____ will you be home?

25. _____ are you going?

26. _____ are you getting there – by bus or train?

27. _____ are you meeting today?

Complete the story with the words in the box.

| jumps | runs | waits | watches | chases |

The little mouse 28. _____ away from the cat.

It is scared of the big, furry cat. The cat 29. _____

for the mouse every day. It looks at and 30. _____

the little hole in the wall. When the mouse comes out,

the cat 31. _____ it around. The cat

32. _____ on the chair and looks around. Where

can the little mouse be?

Write the sentences and questions in the correct order.

33. Pam in the park. jogs

_____

34. sees She stray cat. a

_____

35. She the cat home. brings

_____

36. Can I the cat? keep

_____

37. What does say? her mother

_____

38. Where she can put it?

_____

39. Pam the cat. looks after

_____

40. Does   her brother   cats?   like

_____

41. the cat.   Tim helps   feed   to

_____

42. Tim and Pam   together.   bathe   the cat

_____

_____

Answer Key

Page 5
1. The
2. The
3. The
4. A
5. Mark
6. The
7. She

Page 6
1. The cat sat on the mat.
2. The girl runs.
3. I can see a mouse.
4. The dog sees the cat.
5. I see a boy.
6. The cat sleeps.

Page 7
1. The
2. Jan
3. Ants
4. My
5. I
6. Snuffles

Page 8
Ensure the period is circled for each sentence.
5. I go to school with Tina.
6. Tina is my friend.
7. Danny is our friend.

Page 9
Ensure a period is added at the end of each sentence.
5. I have fun in school.
6. We play games in school.
7. I like my teachers.

Page 10
1. Miss Gray is my teacher.
2. School is fun.
3. I like the playground.
4. Tina and I like the see-saw.
5. Danny likes the swing.

Page 11
Ensure every I is circled for Questions 1–4.
Ensure each blank is filled with a capital I for Questions 5–8.

Page 12
1. I like to read.
2. I can hop and I can jump.
3. My brother and I like to swim.
4. Jake and I have fun together.
Accept all reasonable answers.

Page 13
1. I have fun in the sun.
2. Jake and I play with the beach ball.
3. I like the beach.
4. Peter and I build sandcastles.
5. My dog and I run on the sand.

Page 14
January / February / March / April / May / June / July / August / September / October / November / December

Sunday / Tuesday / Wednesday / Thursday / Friday / Saturday

Page 15
1. I start school on Monday, 3 January.
2. My brother's birthday is in August.
3. We visit my grandparents every Sunday.
4. The months of June and July are very warm.
5. We will celebrate my birthday on a Saturday in September.

Page 16
1. Thursday
2. Wednesday
3. February
4. January
5. Sunday
6. Tuesday

Page 17
1. Dan, Jan, Hill Park
2. Felix
3. Grange Lake
4. Grange Lake, Hill Park
5. My dog is Buster and my cat is Felix.
6. My brother's name is Gary and I am Sue.
7. We stay on Margaret Drive.

Page 18
1. Anne
2. Jim
3. Snowball
4. Candy Road
5. Sweet House
Accept all reasonable answers.

Page 19
1. Don, Marie
2. Pink Hill
3. Mopy, Dopy
4. Pink Hill, Jam Street
5. Don, Marie, James
6. James

Page 20
1. boys, house
2. toys
3. toys, garden
4. garden, house
5. sister

Ensure the correct sentence is matched with each picture.

Page 21
1. van
2. cat, mat
3. hill
4. picnic

Accept all reasonable answers.

Page 22
1. cat
2. rat
3. map
4. van
5. fan
6. house

Page 23
Common nouns: house, teacher, lake, rabbit, rose, flower, cat, mother, mat,
Proper nouns: Anna, Buster, Park Lane, Jake, Janice, Rigby Garden, City Beach

Page 24
1. Circle: friends; Underline: James, John
2. Circle: toys, food
3. Circle: block; Underline: Cross Street
4. Underline: Cameron Primary School
5. Circle: dogs; Underline: James, John
6. Circle: dogs, park, block
7. Circle: park; Underline: Hyde Park

Page 25
1. cat
2. fish
3. bed
4. Mary
5. Maxwell Road
6. Rose

Page 26
1. cat – cats
2. girl – girls
3. boy – boys
4. egg – eggs
5. pencil – pencils
6. book – books
7. bag – bags
8. car – cars
9. hats
10. dolls
11. eyes, ears
12. skirts

Page 27
1. cats
2. bags
3. caps
4. books
5. balls
6. cars

Page 28
1. girl
2. cake
3. room
4. spoons
5. plates, bowls
6. chairs

Page 29
1. a
2. a
3. a
4. an
5. an
6. an
7. an
8. an

Page 30
1. I see an owl in a tree.
2. She cracked an egg into a bowl.
3. We sit in a car and sing a song.
4. May I have an ice cream and a waffle please?
5. He wants an umbrella and a raincoat.

Page 31
1. a
2. a
3. a
4. a
5. an
6. a
7. a
8. an

Page 32
Masculine nouns: boy, king, prince, waiter, father, man, son, uncle, actor, nephew
Feminine nouns: girl, princess, woman, queen, mother, waitress, daughter, aunt, actress, niece

Page 33
Insert correct labels in the picture.

Page 34
1. princess
2. waiter
3. grandmother
4. actor
5. boy

Page 35
1. jumps
2. slides
3. play
4. sits
5. swings
6. skip
7. climbs
8. sleeps

Page 36
1. runs
2. sweeps
3. sit
4. wipes
5. mops

Page 37
1. sit
2. runs
3. sleeps
4. digs
5. play
6. walks

Page 38
1. The cat jumps.
2. The bus moves quickly.
3. Bill paints a picture.
4. Tom likes to read.
5. Jessie plants flowers.

Page 39
1. Janet reads a book.
2. Jack walks up the hill.
3. The elephant moves slowly.
4. The dog chases after the cat.
5. He looks at the boy.
6. Maggie sleeps on the bed.

78

Page 40
1. The cat sits on a mat.
2. The girls like jam.
3. Jacob eats a banana.
4. Thomas walks to school.
5. Jessie plucks flowers.

Page 41
2. Circle: She; <u>Mother</u>
3. Circle: They; <u>The Carrolls</u>
4. Circle: They; <u>The Carrolls and Wendell</u>
5. Circle: They; <u>The Carrolls and Wendell</u>
6. Circle: He; <u>Wendell</u>

Page 42
1. It
2. They
3. It
4. she
5. He

Page 43
1. Max's mother
2. Max
3. The room
4. She
5. They
6. He
7. It

Page 44
1. is
2. are
3. are
4. is
5. am

Page 45
1. is
2. is
3. are
4. are
5. am
6. are
7. are
8. is

Page 46
1. are
2. am
3. are
4. are
5. is
6. is
7. is

Page 47
1. eats, drinks
2. opens
3. sip
4. march
5. chases
6. plays
7. slithers
8. screams

Page 48
1. jumps
2. runs
3. slides
4. sleep
5. drinks
6. kick
7. walk
8. eat
9. play
10. sits

Page 49
1. kicks
2. cycle
3. throws
4. hops
5. wash
6. sit

Page 50
2. George
3. May
4. Alex
6. juice
7. the floor
8. the table

Page 51
1. Underline: Mr Tuck; Circle: the newspapers
2. Underline: Mrs Tuck; Circle: breakfast
3. Underline: Mary; Circle: the juice
4. Underline: Alex; Circle: the table
5. Underline: Margie; Circle: the rabbit
6. Underline: The rabbit; Circle: the carrots
7. Underline: Baby Boo; Circle: his milk
8. Underline: Baby Sue; Circle: the rattle

Accept all reasonable answers.

Page 52
1. The man rocks the boat.
2. She kicks the pail.
3. They bake bread.
4. Mrs Kim stirs the soup.
5. Mr Wendell moves the furniture.
6. Adam plays his guitar.

Page 53
1. is
2. eat
3. milks
4. wears
5. keeps
6. irons
7. drives

Page 54
1. is
2. trains
3. bats
4. catches
5. helps
6. jogs
7. drinks
8. eats

Page 55
1. sings
2. plays
3. claps
4. win
5. stand
6. gives
7. are
8. get
9. presents
10. shakes

Page 56
Ensure the first letter of each sentence is underlined and the period at the end of each sentence is circled.

Underline sentences 5 and 7.

Page 57
1. She sells shells in her shop.
2. There are big shells and small shells.
3. She gets them from the beach.
4. She strings them to make necklaces.
5. She opens her shop early in the morning.
6. She closes the shop late at night.

Page 58
1. You can water the flowers.
2. The flowers are blooming well.
3. There are red and white roses in the garden.
4. The flowers are beautiful.
5. I can give you some roses.
6. You can put them in the vase.
7. I have fruit trees too.
8. I have apple trees and lemon trees.

Page 59
Ensure the first letter of each sentence is underlined and the question mark at the end of each question is circled.

Underline sentences 6 and 7.

Page 60
1. Where are they going?
2. Who are they going out with?
3. Will they return home by dinnertime?
4. What are they going to buy?
5. Can they buy something for me?
6. Do you want to go with them?

Page 61
1. Where can I buy this book?
2. Do you have this book here?
3. Is this the book you want?
4. How much is this book?
5. What book are you looking for?
6. What is the writer's name?
7. Do you have books by Lyndon Wells?
8. Can I have a look at it?

Page 62
1. What   2. Who   3. Where
4. When   5. How   6. a place
7. a person   8. a date

Page 63
1. What   2. Who   3. Where
4. When   5. How

Page 64
1. When   2. What   3. Who
4. Where   5. How   6. When

Page 65
1. The king is sad.
2. Tell the king to come.
3. Shall we cheer him up?
4. He likes to eat cake.
5. Shall we bake him a cake?
6. We can bake him a strawberry cake.

Page 66
1. This bear likes snow.
2. The water is cold.
3. Can the bear swim?
4. The bear swims fast.
5. What color is the bear?

Page 67
1. The boys will play baseball.
2. The baseball smashes the window.
3. The teacher is angry.
4. The teacher scolds the boys.
5. The boys are sorry.

Page 68
1. The, Gruff   2. They, Nosey   3. Nosey
4. Nosey, Toll Bridge
5. Her sister is named Sheila.
6. They have a pet called Muffins.
7. Muffins stays in their house on Park Lane.

Page 69
1. Gruff Park   2. Amy
3. Mr and Mrs Smith   4. Trevor

Page 70
1. Jenny   2. The   3. Gruff
4. Nosey   5. Nosey   6. The

Page 71
1. This month is June.
2. I have a pet goldfish named Chester.
3. Do you know Sylvia?
4. Where is Mrs Smith going?
5. She is going to Prime Park.
6. Does Tom go to school on Saturdays?
7. is   8. eats   9. are
10. keeps   11. are   12. flies
13. sleeps   14. An, a   15. prince
16. nephew   17. grandfather   18. a
19. She   20. They   21. sits, It
22. pull, They   23. run   24. When
25. Where   26. How   27. Who
28. runs   29. waits   30. watches
31. chases   32. jumps
33. Pam jogs in the park.
34. She sees a stray cat.
35. She brings the cat home.
36. Can I keep the cat?
37. What does her mother say?
38. Where can she put it?
39. Pam looks after the cat.
40. Does her brother like cats?
41. Tim helps to feed the cat.
42. Tim and Pam bathe the cat together.